Abundance,
a Journey from
Anxiety and
Depression

JAY SOOKNANAN

BALBOA.
PRESS
A DIVISION OF HAY HOUSE

Balboa Press books may be ordered through booksellers or by contacting:

Balboa Press
A Division of Hay House
1663 Liberty Drive
Bloomington, IN 47403
www.balboapress.com
1 (877) 407-4847

Because of the dynamic nature of the Internet, any web addresses or
links contained in this book may have changed since publication and
may no longer be valid. The views expressed in this work are solely those
of the author and do not necessarily reflect the views of the publisher,
and the publisher hereby disclaims any responsibility for them.

The author of this book does not dispense medical advice or prescribe
the use of any technique as a form of treatment for physical, emotional,
or medical problems without the advice of a physician, either directly
or indirectly. The intent of the author is only to offer information
of a general nature to help you in your quest for emotional and
spiritual well-being. In the event you use any of the information in
this book for yourself, which is your constitutional right, the author
and the publisher assume no responsibility for your actions.

Any people depicted in stock imagery provided by Thinkstock are
models, and such images are being used for illustrative purposes only.
Certain stock imagery © Thinkstock.

Print information available on the last page.

ISBN: 978-1-5043-9032-3 (sc)
ISBN: 978-1-5043-9033-0 (e)

Balboa Press rev. date: 10/18/2017

CONTENTS

INTRO

MY EXPERIENCE

I wrote this book because I was going through anxiety and depression. I put a lot of work into figuring out strategies to overcome these states and live in one of abundance.

My goals were so high and my past was so deep that the thoughts overwhelmed me. I was letting go of my childhood dreams to go after my newfound vision. The transition from letting go of my past and all my struggles to going after even bigger goals gave me anxiety. There was so much to do to achieve my new vision, it was so grand that I was afraid that I could not achieve it, so many doubts swarmed my mind. I just wanted to be able to help people, make good money and provide for my family.

My new vision was bigger than just me and my family and what I wanted. It became me being able to help the world end suffering and for all to live in abundance of opportunity to necessities and room for everyone to flourish in their own dreams. My old dream was disappearing and the new one was taking its place. While choosing this I began to think that if it does not work out, people would look at me as a failure. They would say "You had everything setup to be a doctor. Stick to the plan".

My new plan is to help people and communities to their own well-being practices: of meditation, good nutrition, healthy lifestyles, and then further work on projects in ending hunger, providing shelter, nutrition, clothing, healthcare and education to people without the opportunities, inspiring abundance and love in all. Could I do this? I was unsure and afraid.

My mind was swarmed with thoughts and my body became motionless. I felt I had no time for anything except work; I forgot to allow myself to enjoy my own life. My healthy habits stopped: I stopped working out, I stopped listening to motivational videos, I stopped interacting with my friends and family, I avoided any types of parties or gatherings and I stopped meditating. I felt like I needed to do other things that seemed more important at the time. By not prioritizing my mind and health, my mind ran wild. I felt like I was doing so much, but my situation had not changed. The internal chatter was getting louder and louder and I was losing control. My fear kept rising. Even then, I would still go to work and attend Toastmasters. Every moment I had I would lay in my bed in the dark, drifting in and out of sleep.

My anxiety was increasing because I was not doing what I was "supposed" to do. I was supposed to be increasing my sales, working at my job, growing my business, and doing so many other things that were new to me. I was transitioning from becoming a doctor to working in Real Estate in order to be able to buy my mom a house and help her retire. I hate watching her go to work to do hard labor as a custodian after taking care of 4 children for the past 35 years on her own. She had worked non-stop all her life. I felt like I had the world on my shoulders and I could not hold it up. I understand that my mom is strong and I understand that she sacrificed the last four decades. She raised good kids; I feel it's her turn to have freedom.

I was living in darkness, I worked the night shift and in the daytime, I would stay in my room with the shades closed and the lights off. I was exhausted from lack of sleep for the past year and I was not doing my real estate activities, which I saw as the *only* way to have *my vision* pan out, the way I said it would work, instead of letting my vision come out the way my internal core being wanted it to. Not doing the activities led to me feeling anxiety and that then became depression.

One day, the voice inside my head said "Why don't you kill yourself? If life is so bad, go kill yourself. Jump out the window. The window is right there, jump! Jump right now!" I never thought I would face the concept of suicide.

I got up. I reminded myself that I felt pain before and that I am still here. "Breathe through it. You'll make it," I told myself; life is beautiful and I keep repeating it to try to convince myself. "Jay life is good. Relax and keep going." My self-motivation was weak, but my internal thoughts started to shift away from negative thoughts.

I slowly started meditating, working out, and reading and listening to self-help motivation material again. My mindset was changing, but I was still overwhelmed and depressed, it was not over.

One night, that voice came back and reminded me, "is life so bad? If it is, just jump out the window! Do not think, just jump!"

That is when everything changed. I got up and decided, "Jay you are not going to kill yourself. You have so much going for you. You matter! You are here to do great things! You have helped so many people already and you will continue to do so. Jay, you have affected so many people. You have people that come up and tell you they would not be where they are if it was not for you. You matter, Jay, and you are here to make a difference."

That night, I told myself "Go after your dreams and keep pushing, regardless of the circumstances. I did *not have to* do anything; I *deserve to* live out my dreams for myself, my family, my friends and the world. You've gotten As in the hardest classes, while working, volunteering and joining and building organizations. You have changed your life around for the better, from a teenage life of bad decisions and hanging out with crowds that were poorly influenced to a successful college graduate, working as an EMT in the best hospital, accepted to your masters program, became a Real Estate agent and in your free time you work on your public speaking and leadership skills. This is only the start of the journey. Get up and keep going!"

I am a Health and Wellness coach, teaching yoga, meditation, different exercises and good nutrition. I continue to work in Real Estate seeing the different ways we really help people. I am working to start my first non-profit organization to help people transition from out of the shelter system and back to society. I have learned to balance these responsibilities with my personal life by taking care of my well-being through my meditative practices and good nutrition, allowing me to experience less anxiety and get more into action, keeping my energy and positivity levels high.

This is only the beginning of the journey and I will continue to learn, grow and connect, so we as a team can help more people. We are all part of this universe and together we can end suffering and live in harmony with one another.

CHAPTER 1

Anxiety and Depression

How does anxiety and depression originate?

What are telltale signs that someone may be suffering from anxiety and/or depression?

What resources do we have to support ourselves or someone who may be suffering?

ANXIETY

Anxiety exist the same as any other emotion: stress, happiness, sadness, joy. What we will do is learn how to overcome the feeling and the moment. Anxiety stems from fear. When fear arises, our body instinct is the fight or flight response. This increases our energy use, which drains us both mentally and physically.

National Institute of Mental Health states that "over 40 million people in the United States over the age of 18 suffer from some anxiety related disorder" and that is just those who have been diagnosed.

Anxiety can also stem from stress. Stress originates from external factors such as finances, deadlines, relationship/family issues, school, work, and other responsibilities. These are all things that we, as individuals, have little to no control over. We can only do our part, we cannot control external factors. When our thoughts originate from fear, we end up facing more challenge due to our thoughts become reality. We have to be careful when it comes to how we think and react. We can gain control of our thoughts through practices of our own well-being.

Anxiety and fear originate within us. How can we take control of our fear and anxiety? How can we overcome them and stomp through the stresses of life allowing us to create joy, love and abundance?

Anxiety arises when we are about to do something we may not want to do because of unfamiliarity with the task or past experiences. Even if the events are not directly related, but have similarities that lead our minds to associate them with each other, then that can create anxiety under certain circumstances.

For instance, image a shy young man. Due to him being shy and timid, he lacks confidence to approach a girl. He either approaches her with low self-esteem, which to stems from fear, making her dismiss him or even worse, he does not approach her at all. That feeling of being rejected stays with him throughout life, unless and until he decides to confront that fear.

The same young man goes on to build his clients for his business. Due to that learned behavior and his lack of confidence in himself, he is afraid to talk with new clients and offer his service. The anxiety took over him and he is an unable to build his business, all because of one learned behavior. Then it becomes a vicious cycle, that anxiety will prevent him from taking advantages of opportunities and these missed opportunities will enable his anxiety and eventually he will end up in a state of depression.

This is just one example, but how many times are we put into situations where at first, we would not want to do the task at hand and then we let hesitation, fear, and anxiety build up? If we let the cycle continue, we then become paralyzed and unable to grow. If you are not growing and learning you are, ultimately, dying.

As stated before, anxiety activates the fight or flight responses of the brain, which heightens our sense of awareness and keeps us alert. This is perfect for if you're climbing up the side of mountain or standing on the edge of a steep cliff, but if that anxiety persists, it can become detrimental: we will lose all our energy reserves and BOOM, everything comes crashing down.

This is situational anxiety, this can be overcome when we confront the fear, use our courage, and attack the situation in front of us. What's the worst that can happen? The girl says no, or that client doesn't need your services at this moment? Through experiential learning, the more we confront these situations the better our outcomes. Every time we do confront a situation that we fear, we build confidence, such as stage fright. The more we get up there the more we get comfortable and learn techniques to perform with more excitement and less nervousness. When we accept the challenge or the obstacle placed in front of us and we get out of our comfort zone. That widens our comfort zone which makes it easier to continue extending it further, allowing us to reach our highest potential and live the life we dream of. I lived with situational anxiety I could not build by business because I was afraid to offer my services in real estate and of being rejected. The anxiety built and led to depression because I didn't confront my fear; instead I just let it sit and fester in my mind. I ended up spending months not building my business, always finding something more "important" to do. When I started practicing my meditative rituals, I overcame the fear for a few moments at a time. I started to work past this obstacle and I made my first sale in the first two weeks. The thing is, if I stopped accepting the challenge my wall of fear would build up again, so I learned to continuously push myself and expand my comfort zone.

Another type of anxiety is generalized anxiety that is long lasting. People with this disorder do not even realize they are experiencing anxiety. They have lived in this state for so long that it has become their way of life. Their instinct in any event is to worry. General anxiety can originate from genetics, abnormal brain patterns, environmental factors, trauma and stressful events, abuse, death of loved ones, divorce and change in general.

Common symptoms may be excessive, continuous worry, unrealistic view of problems, restlessness, feeling on edge, irritability, muscle tension, headaches, sweating, difficulty concentrating, nausea, frequent bathroom use, trouble sleeping, tiredness and being easily startled.

Steps to overcoming anxiety are practicing, relaxation techniques listening to music, meditating, exercising and other rituals specific to you personally that seem to help and/or show positive results.

My practices include all relaxation techniques mentioned in the next chapter. Sometimes I use music; other practices that I do daily is meditate, exercise, and chanting. This helps me to stay centered, helping control my reactions and emotions. By staying centered, I remember that we are all one and nothing can work if we do not work together. This promotes me in being humble and grateful, allowing me to live with compassion for everyone.

Depression can arise from many different faculties such as biological, unbalanced amount of chemicals in the brain or cognitive reasons, such as negative thinking or low self-esteem. Negative thinking will persist when feeling anxious. Women are twice as likely to suffer from depression as men are due to menopause, menstruation, pregnancy, childbirth and certain hormonal imbalances. Depression may also coincide with other illnesses, such as Parkinson's, Alzheimer's, diabetes and medication side effects. It can also come from genetics or from situational difficulties such as life events, financial difficulties, death, and divorce.

Symptoms of depression are persistent anxiousness, sadness and feeling of emptiness and no connection with the world. A person may be sleeping too much or too little, have eating issues, either gaining or losing excessive weight, difficulty remembering or making decisions, fatigue and loss of energy, feelings of guilt, hopelessness or worthlessness, headaches, chronic pain, and thoughts of suicide and death.

Treatments maybe psychotherapy and support groups, positive self-talks, and positive group talks. To treat depression down to its base, we must recognize negative thought patterns and rewrite the thinking pattern that led to that state. Anti-depression drugs help control the chemical balance in the brain to treat depression, but it is not a permanent solution unless you stay on medication.

Things you can do to help yourself while in a state of depression:

- Allow others to help you achieve goals
- Participate in activities you enjoy
- Exercise moderately

- Remember you can and will get past your depression
- Be around people that you feel comfortable confiding in
- Set goals that are realistic to achieve in the time given

The National Institute of Mental Health Support line:
(866) 615-6464

I believe depression sets in when we are overwhelmed. We feel we have to do so much and the stress of it all paralyzes our mind, preventing us from doing even minimal task, throughout the day. Our thoughts are running wild, so we feel like we have no time for ourselves or for the things important to us and our well-being such as meditation, exercise, spending time with family and friends, or relaxation.

The way I overcame my depression was first, I had to get out the paralyses of my mind. This was the most difficult step. After a lot of internal work, I started to take action! Sure, do the pre-requisites; plan, figure out what is needed for what you want and go. Stop waiting and stop thinking so much. Just go out there and get the task done. If I fear a task or it is the hardest one, tackle that first. When I slowly started hitting goals, I built momentum and started overcoming my anxiety and depression.

Things you can do to help you take control of your mind, and prevent yourself from becoming overwhelmed are exercising, meditating and all its variations, chanting, positive affirmations, positive thinking, practice of gratitude and other things that will be explained in the coming chapters.

CHAPTER 2

Meditative Practices

Meditation/ Chanting/ Gratitude/ Exercises

Benefits

How to implement them

Meditative practices include deep breathing meditation, observation of the breath, visualization, chanting, the practice of gratitude and the most physically active exercise. Meditative practices can be applied in any activity you are doing, by reducing your focus solely to the task at hand and your breath. Whatever you may be doing, such as listening to a lecture, reading your emails, or walking, you can reduce your distractions by enhancing your concentration on what you are doing and on your breath, aiding in focus and reducing internal and external chatter. Here I will highlight a few meditative practices and their benefits.

MEDITATION

What is meditation? It looks simple, right? You just sit there, put your hands on your lap, and that's it. Looks can be deceiving. It is not just sitting there doing nothing. Meditation is *active* training of the mind. Meditation helps create mindfulness, compassion, wisdom, concentration, inner strength and resilience. There are many different types of meditation you could try: visualization, mantras, observing the breath, and deep breathing.

Meditation may look simple, but we all encounter thoughts racing around in our mind, going on ifs, ands, buts and so many other thoughts. The mind goes on a default mode network, "The DMN is "on" or active when we're not thinking about anything in particular, when our minds are just wandering from thought to thought. The 60,000 thoughts per day Dr. Wayne Dyer talked about, that are 90% repetitive!" -Forbes. Dr. Wayne Dyer states we think on average 60,000 thoughts a day and with practice of meditation we can reduce them to 200 thoughts focusing on what is most important to us.

The clarity of mind helps with time management, getting things in order, and finding solutions rather quickly. When a challenge or obstacle arises I am ready and don't think "why me?" Instead, I think, "how can I solve this problem or complete this task?" Let's get into the logistics of meditation.

First meditation requires time and commitment. I run a meditation class and the biggest objection I hear is "I do not have time." Who owns your time? A financial advisor will always tell you pay yourself first, before spending any money. Meditation is equivalent to paying yourself giving yourself your energy to center yourself.

Meditation gives us time, it does not steal our time. Studies how that when stressed or anxious, we retain less information and what we study is harder to remember. That few minutes we take to meditate allows us to comprehend more and make more connections than we would have without it. It is shown that a person who meditates can deal with more complex situations as well, due to the developing of cerebral matter that happens while meditating.

Proven benefits of meditation are: reduced stress, improved concentration, healthier lifestyle, increased self-awareness, increased happiness, emotional well-being, better time management, amongst other things that are better understood when you actually experience them. This is proven through many university studies and through my own lived experience. During my first two years of college, I was a full-time student, on the dean's list, while working full-time and maintaining good relationships. I then went onto research, taking courses outside of school, working and volunteering, while being a diligent student. I am not trying to brag, I am saying that I understand the challenges that people may face and meditation really helped me get through these challenges in an efficient and pleasant manner, still maintaining my joy and not losing sight of the importance of my family and friends.

The first challenge people face when meditating are their thoughts are overpowering their ability to clear their mind. Focus on your breath. Inhale slow and deep, bring the breath to your forehead and hold it. Then slowly release it and push it all the way out. The thoughts will come and, when they do, focus on them one at a time. There are three types of thoughts that will come up. Future, thoughts of what you have to do. When they arise take the time to create a plan of action and then go back to focusing on your breath. The next is the past. It is something that has already occurred that you cannot change. Maybe you have to forgive yourself or someone else for something that affected you or another; if so, do it right there in that moment. Forgive and let it go. Understand that you are not going backwards; we decide from this point how we move forward. I have forgiven myself and my past friends for endeavors we went through together. When I forgave them, subconsciously, I was able to wish good thoughts for them and hope they had the best outcomes. After settlement of that thought, move on and come back to the breath. The third is a tangent or a repetitive thought that does not need to be explored now. When you become aware of the thought, ask yourself is this necessary to explore right now, if not go back to the breath. Ultimately, we want to focus on the breath, but major, powerful thoughts are very persistent and we get to handle them, right here.

The second challenge is the time commitment. Set a schedule and stick to it, which is easier said than done. When you see the benefits, you will make the time. What is holding you back? Is the practice difficult? Lets continue to look at strategies to keep us focused.

Another challenge is people nod off. Sometimes your mind and body need the rest, so do not beat yourself up if you fall asleep. We live in a fast-paced society, where information is thrown at us and we are bombarded by social media. Sleeping is not meditation though, so when you are well-rested, try again. If you find yourself continuously nodding off, put some energy into it. Fix your posture, lengthen your spine, lift your crown, pick up your chin, broaden your shoulders and contract your abdomen. If you are still nodding off, get up and do a slow meditative walk, being aware of all your movements, while focusing on your breathing. When you lose focus always revert back to your meditation practice, breathing, visualization or your mantra.

Another challenge is stillness, pain may arise, it is a sensation, no matter how painful, when you realize it is just a sensation, you will be able not to shift posture as much.

If temperature is affecting your practice, adjust clothing appropriately to the surrounding atmosphere.

The last major difficulty some people encounter is that they cannot relax. In order to help yourself relax in preparation of meditation you must learn to find ways to dissipate your energy, may it be exercise, listening to music, walking, and talking with someone and then slowly come back to meditation.

Practice helps to bring compassion, patience, wisdom, resilience, and strength. Continuous practice helps you enter deeper into your subconscious thoughts, where you realize your strength and wisdom allowing you to develop the thoughts most important to you.

It has shown me that we are one vessel in this universe and that we all work together. When we release all our wants and desires the universe allows us to play the role we need to in order to further help humanity and live the life that we dream of.

CHANTING

Chanting creates a vibration. Your sound creates frequency. Some people chant Om- which is said to be the same frequency as everything in nature. Everything in nature has a vibration and we become connected through our vibrations.

Chanting has meditative effects because the vibration and rhythm help to slow down the nervous system and calm the mind as well as help reduce blood pressure. Chanting helps to reduce anxiety and depression by connecting the body-mind circuit through vibration which reduces stress and alleviates the endocrine system and the nervous system.

Chanting is proven to clear away subconscious patterns, helping to rewrite all the things the world has put into our mind from a young age from music, television, books to the things taught to us by our teachers, our parents, our bosses, and any other influences of society. Chanting allows us to override all of that, down to a subconscious level and break away from the walls that society has put our minds in. This helps us to think outside the box.

Chanting is soothing and helps reduce mind chatter. It helps connect us to the world, allowing us to realize we are one. By connecting our mind and heart, we align ourselves with the universe and we allow ourselves to come into our inner being, experiencing joy and compassion and reducing envy and pride.

Chanting boosts immunity, it's free, and best of all we can implement it anywhere: while driving, walking, and even sitting on the train. It's especially good for places we may feel uncomfortable with closing your eyes and meditating.

Chanting allows the calming of the mind. Our voice empowers us and opens our intuition; it also helps increase radiance of our thoughts through, scientific phenomenon. Remember, all sound is vibration. Those thoughts in your mind get refined, reducing the noise, allowing our deep core thoughts to come to the surface and connect with the divine nature. I have seen that the more I chant, the more my thoughts manifest. I want a parking spot, boom. I was thinking of a person and they called. When visualizing, which visualizing is a thought, I see things come to fruition. I see this book impacting a million lives.

GRATITUDE

Gratitude is the quality of being thankful, appreciative and kind.

Gratitude is a sense of appreciation, showing yourself the positive in all aspects of life.

Gratitude allows us to become more optimistic, letting good vibes run through and around us.

Practicing gratitude has been shown to help you sleep better, be happier, and exercise more regularly.

Studies show people who keep a gratitude journal have a heightened sense of determination, attention, enthusiasm, energy, and optimism. Gratitude also reduces pains, aliments, and aches.

A 2012 Chinese study reported in Psychology Today shows keeping a gratitude journal trumps sleep levels. People suffer less from depression and anxiety when practicing gratitude; sleep has less of an effect on anxiety and depression levels.

Gratitude releases dopamine, giving you that feel-good experience.

Since the practice helps us appreciate our life more and gives us a positive perspective, it helps lower any anxiety and depression you may have. I started practicing gratitude a few months ago and my life has changed dramatically, both physically and mentally. I use the mala beads given to me by Venerable Geneva. On every bead, there are 108, I say something I am grateful for every night: friends, family, space, food, breathing, being able to walk, and my clothes just to name a few. I have found an awesome woman, my relationships have become stronger with my friends and family and my optimism has allowed me to stop playing small and go out and live the life I want. My living area has gotten clearer and my positivity has risen. I see more opportunities everyday to help me achieve my purpose and continue to create a brighter vision.

Gratitude improves your hypothalamus, a control center of your brain, which allows your body to perform better, and regulates hunger, sleep, body temperature, growth, and metabolism.

Gratitude helps in the process of resisting stress, which means increasing resilience to bad situations. It eases your mind and allows you to fall asleep more easily and, brings more positive emotions.

Ways to incorporate gratitude into your daily life is to stop and look at life from a point of gratefulness. Have a gratitude journal where you write at least one thing that you are grateful for everyday. When you have a negative thought, observe it and then change your view to something positive about the situation. Give out compliments and share stories of appreciation with those around you. Work to not complain, gossip or criticize. When talking with others be genuine and happy. Lastly, join a cause important to you, where you donate money, time or talent.

There are many ways to increase your practice of gratitude: slow down and savor life's moments, experience things, listen to music that reflects how you feel, write a letter to your younger self sending your wisdom and then use the wisdom that you send your younger self in your life now, acknowledge highlights of your month, make a list of all the difficult situations you overcame, fall asleep saying things you are grateful for. An old saying is, when in doubt focus out, meaning let go of thinking about you and focus on others. Do something good for someone else, write a letter or treat someone to coffee, any act of kindness for someone else. Another powerful technique is a gratitude rock. You carry it with you and place it on your desk when working or whenever you need to remind yourself to be grateful.

I encourage you to do the highlights of your life, do monthly highlights as well and difficult situations you have overcome as well.

My note to my younger self:

Dear Younger Self,

What is the worst thing that can happen?
Remember you can always get back up! Breathe. Breathing will get you through any pain.
Enjoy your journey, love whatever you are doing, and pace yourself.
Don't be scared to be coached by others, especially when they have your best interests at heart. Go for it! Don't be scared to talk to women or to anyone at all. Know you are deserving of what you want. You are a gift. You are unique. You are powerful beyond your belief. Stay humble. Stay respectful. Keep your manners high. Love everyone, and most of all, love yourself, the person you are, your big heart. Do not be scared of changing for the better. If you are determined to be successful then you will be.
Tell me one time you did not make it through the hard times. You are someone that becomes aware and learns. You get to choose who you want to be, what you want to do! You matter and should get all you deserve! You do not have to do anything, you get to. You get the chance to achieve your wildest dreams.

Gratitude helps you enjoy the moments and be more present in life.

Gratitude has made me more positive allowing me to change my internal dialogue. Negative thoughts that may have risen before dissipate. Being positive changes my view of life and allows more beauty to continuously enter in my journey. Things I may have taken for granted are now so much appreciated, as simple as being able to have a conversation with my sister or mother.

EXERCISE

Exercise too can be a meditative process. When exercise gets your attention, and you give the process your full attention, your focus increases. You are eliminating the distractions and noise of the outside. That allows you to come in to the present moment and be aware of your thoughts, as well.

Exercise helps reduce stress and increases concentration with the help of bodily chemicals. Exercise gives you natural happiness because your body produces endorphins, which are the body's natural painkillers.

Right after a workout session, your self-esteem is boosted and your self-image is improved. Regardless of how we may look at that moment in time, when we finish the exercise the feeling of self-worth increases and we feel more attractive. Knowing we are working on ourselves, and the release of endorphins give you a feeling of euphoria, helping let go of any doubt and fear in you. Showing us we can do anything we put our mind to.

Exercise does not have to be in a cold dark gym, we can be exercising outdoors enjoying nature, and connecting with the world. Exercising outdoors allows us more freedom, we could jog, play sports, bike, rock climb, hike, canoe, ski and so many other things that maybe more fun than just running on a treadmill or lifting weights. Don't get me wrong, I love the gym and making my workouts fun, I'm just saying that we have other options.

Exercise boosts chemicals in the brain to reduce degeneration of the hippocampus. The hippocampus is responsible for memory and learning. Stress is reduced through exercise, alleviating us from anxiety. Exercise has been shown to help the development of brain derived protein, which helps us with decision making capabilities, higher levels of thinking, and enhances our learning abilities. *The brain comes with the bronze.*

Exercise releases dopamine, the feel-good chemical, in the brain. Dopamine is also released when we indulge in pleasures such as sex, drugs, alcohol, and food. Exercise can be our outlet away from addiction, especially since both activities release the same chemicals. Exercise lets you become more relaxed, allowing for better sleeping patterns when practiced at appropriate times. We get to feel more comfortable inside our own skin.

When I turned 22, I started exercising more consistently and purposefully. I transitioned from my first major breakup with my first girlfriend; we were together for four years and we had a history of drinking and smoking. I used exercise to help me push the past away and get over my addictions. I started working out and the release of dopamine helped me to control myself around other pleasures such as drugs, alcohol, food, or sex. I got healthier, had more confidence, and even slept better.

I was 195 lbs. at that time which was thirty pounds overweight for someone my height. I am now in the appropriate 165 lbs. range. I feel great and now have exercise in my daily and weekly regime. Exercising has helped sharpen my mind and views on life. It gave me perspective and I see the world from a different light and different ways you can help people through exercise.

Since our mind becomes sharper when exercising, our productivity increases and for the next two hours our sense of creativity is heightened as well. Take a run or go have a good workout session before you create your next masterpiece.

Best of all, with exercise, we get to inspire others. We can work out with our buddies, which helps with creating connections and healthy communities. It is shown that our pain tolerance increases when working as a team, so you can actually go further with others.

I exercise anytime I have a chance but I feel the morning is the best because we get the blood moving to drive us through the day. Experts say the best time to exercise is midday, because it gives you that second wind. Late afternoons work as well. Right before bed may affect our sleep because our mind will be more sharp and active, but it can also exhaust you and knock you out. Individually we can determine what time is best for us. We can ask ourselves, "How can exercise bring more energy to my life and to my day? Where should I place it in my schedule for the optimal use?"

Duration of exercise recommended weekly is 150 minutes for moderate exercise and 75 minutes for vigorous. When we break it down, that is 5 days of 15 to 30 minutes of exercise per day. Imagine 15 minutes a day will sharpen your mind, make your smarter, sexier, more creative, happier, reduce stress, help inspire others, and help you overcome your addictions.

Choose what exercise works for you. There are many options and new innovative classes that are out: Run, HITT, CrossFit, Kickboxing, sports, and outdoor activities. We get to have fun with our workouts; we could be learning a dance or a martial art, and connect with friends to create positive habits together.

There are many different meditative practices highlighted in this chapter, pick one or a few. Do whatever works for you. I practice all of them, some daily and some weekly. It helps keep my energy up. Meditation has given me time management, wisdom, patience, and a connection with the universe. Chanting has let my visions and thoughts come to fruition much more readily. Focused exercise destroys outside stressors and raises my confidence. The combination allows me to live in an abundant state. These meditative practices help elevate and regulate my energy, and allow me to go live the extraordinary life I dream of having.

CHAPTER 3

Find your Purpose

What goals do you have in all areas of life

Create your vision towards it

Affirm the dream, remember it and strive towards it

When you have a purpose, you are able to see what aligns with your vision and what doesn't. It helps you when you are in that moment of indecision. Remembering the life you want and dream of will help guide your decisions. Your purpose supports you in avoiding the nonsense and the things you do not want in your life. We all have different purposes, which we can see by all the different people and the lives they lead. Even though as a universe we are all one, we each have different roles. Let's work on some steps to finding your purpose.

First set aside some time to allow your true intuition to flow out of you. Remember we are all one, allowing us access to all the resources in this universe. The realization shows us our abundance. We are all connected, so we all have access to all the resources in the world. A major tool to access all the resources we need is the ability to *ask* for them. We have the power to show others our vision and see who else's vision aligns with ours. By connecting with one another our access to resources increase and abundance becomes infinite. Once we realize we have access to all the resources in the world, we can move forward.

Next is to settle in the mindset of abundance realizing there is more than enough of everything. Now think from the higher self, with no limitations. What do you want to do in this world? How do you want to help your family, your friends, your community and yourself? Remember, you count and you are part of this world.

Ask yourself, "What would I do with all my potential and access to all the resources of the world? What would my purpose be?"

Take your time and let it flow on to the paper, let it come from your higher being where there are no limitations, no fear, no doubt, and a high sense of faith. Just write, you can always change it later. Get something on the paper so you have somewhere to start.

Now that you have your purpose written, look at what you wrote. Examine the language, allow your purpose to be broad yet meaningful. Allow your wildest dreams to come to fruition. Remember, life will change and so may your vision. The purpose will support you in staying directed and allow your inner drive to take over when the challenges arise and you may want to give up on your dreams.

My purpose is to help the world come together to end suffering of humanity and to save the planet from our own destruction. I will gain support through my networks and different endeavors to create systems and work with others to promote nutrition, water, education, healthcare and other opportunities to all people. Throughout my life I will work to inspire the young, people who have given up and any of those I may motivate. Ultimately, I want to make sure my family is supported and have what they want.

Your view may be grand and you may start questioning if you can really do this or how is this even possible. You would not have the thought, if you could not manifest it. Do not let your dreams overwhelm you. Come back inside your being and feel your connectedness to the world and be in a place of freedom, bliss, opportunities, and joy.

Remember you are powerful, you have great potential, and, best of all you do not have to do it all by yourself. You have the universe to support you. You get to *ask* for what you *want*.

Now we can figure out the ways of getting to our end goals. What can we do to make our vision come true?

My purpose has been becoming more directed and my vision has been expanding through my continuous growth and by taking actions towards my dreams. I continue to see more of what I want in the world and how I can help. I continue to grow in clarity and see things come to fruition. The reason I express this is to remind you, our purpose, when written down, is not etched in stone and permanent, we get to change it to what our deepest desires reveal. Our vision will continue to manifest as we travel our path. We will learn what we want and what we do not want and work towards it.

Do not change it because you think your goals are unachievable, change it only if you see new things that better fit the outcome you want to achieve.

Stand in your vision. Do not let the challenges that arise push you around. Stand in your power! Make what you want happen!

23

At some points in the journey you may think, why even go after this purpose and goal? For this reason, we have to develop our Big Why: Why do we want to achieve this vision? Let's give ourselves the reasons to keep going. Is it something you are doing for your family, is it for your happiness and to fulfill your dreams, is it for the community and the world? What is your Big Why? What is the reason you get out of bed and keep going?

My Big Why is I choose to live in a continuous state of abundance, and to help my family, friends and the world reach a mindset of abundance as well. I choose to travel, enjoy my journey, have vacations, eat with my community, and continue to grow and learn how to help more people. I choose to help end suffering and gain access to opportunities such as health, nutrition, water, clothing, education and shelter for all.

My BIG WHY

_____
_____
_____
_____
_____
_____
_____
_____
_____
_____
_____
_____
_____
_____

Next, when the mission seems impossible or you are stuck, lets ask:

What can I do to have this vision turnout? Who could I enroll in this vision?

Remember we are all one and the universe, including all its people, are here to support.

Some questions to ask yourself:

"How can I achieve my goals and dreams?"

_____

_____

_____

_____

_____

(ex. Real estate, investments, networking, continuously learning, good habits and working on skills)

"What may get in the way of my vision and how can I prevent that from happening?"

_____

_____

_____

_____

_____

(ex. Procrastination, laziness, not staying focused, letting others rule my agenda.)

Keep your purpose and vision in your face, on your phone, on your wall and let it drive you.

Make your vision more detailed to help you increase clarity and allow you to know exactly what you want.

To manifest your vision, time spent visualizing helps bring it to reality. Sit down and meditate, eyes close and picture what you want: the house and the joyous activities you could be doing in it, that dream vacation and feeling the abundance of joy, the numerous events on your bucket list, that giant crowd coming out to see you or all the people you see receiving food, shelter, education, and healthcare, and the gratitude it brings to them and yourself.

Take 5 minutes every day to visualize your dreams and that will turn them into reality.

A vision board can support in enhancing anyone's vision. A vision board is pictures of what you want and affirmations on the goal to help reach your mind at a subconscious level. We can create vision boards for every aspect of life, health, well-being, family, friends, vacations, and whatever else that may be important to you.

Hang the vision boards around your house and office. Put it on your screen savers and wallpapers. Reclaim control over your mind and feed yourself the thoughts you want to come to fruition.

I have three vision boards in my room, a board of appreciation with my friends and family, my first vision board attracting all the material things I want, and one of words of empowerment with a dry-erase board where I write my goals.

GOALS

Start getting more specific with goals to help you reach your vision. Attach emotions to your goals because dreams and goals alone can get cold and just become another checklist. Look at all your categories of life: friends, family, finances, career, education, health, spirituality, and ways you may want to help your community. Break down your goals for each category annually, quarterly, monthly, weekly, and daily.

Take your time, and enjoy the journey.

Do not let goals overwhelm you. Decide that your goals will turn out. Ask yourself "How can I reach these goals and enjoy myself?" State outcomes and let the universe decide how you will get there. Be open, present, and connected with the universe and put in the work that your intuition tells you to.

AFFIRMING GOALS

Keep your goals surrounding you: pictures everywhere, goals written down and reviewed frequently, screen savers, strong affirmations, joyous moments of life, your vision boards, and people you may aspire to be. Have these things in your home, your office, and even your bathroom if you want.

Fill your mind with your goals and ambitions. Use autosuggestion, statements and pictures repeated of an outcome you desire to hit your mind subconsciously. Have a reminder of why you are doing any activity in front of you to keep you going. Attach your vision to emotions; how would completing the vision or goal make you feel? What will you be bringing to the table for others? I would like to help my mom retire and get her a house; that will make me happy and give me a sense of contribution. I would like to setup systems to ensue that we join together to end suffering; that, too, will bring me a sense of joy and contribution as well as fulfill my greatest dream.

Lock in that vision, keep your eye on the target, and recalculate when needed. We have made it this far and we are only going to keep on going.

CHAPTER 4

Morals and Principles

Lets determine our morals and principles

Revaluate ideas about money

Remove associate between class and morality

Decide what are your principles and morals

My morals and principles are very important for me and lay a key foundation for anything I may do in life. I work in my highest integrity because my name means a great deal to me. I will not tarnish my name for advances because I value the trust and my name represents.

We do not want anything to come in our way and jeopardize our vision. We want to build our vision on a strong foundation. We need to determine our moral and principles that we choose to live by.

The foundation of morality and principles is key because the world will challenge us. The world will challenge our character and integrity and see exactly how far we will go to have what we want. Are you going to do anything to achieve your dream, even if it's immoral, ultimately building your legacy on a poor foundation? Are you going to forget your family and friends, the ones who supported you in the toughest of times? Are you going to do things falsely, or make faulty products that appear good? Will you be so dedicated to work that you forget your friends and family? Will you lose sleep for your goals or your social life? Will you rob people who are naïve and unaware to make a dollar? We all have choices, what will you do to achieve your dreams and have your vision come to fruition?

What foundation will you build? What morals and principles will you live by?

My principles are:

- Have an open mind and strong determination.
- Live with integrity, meaning to do the right thing even when no one is looking.
- Be considerate, because I never know what someone else may be going through.
- Have manners and respect for all; we get to decide what role we want to play in every relationship we are in, parent-child, boss-employee, friend to friend.
- Be humble, with all our successes we have to remember we are all one.
- Enjoy life, do not get bogged down with goals and achievements, that you forget to enjoy the moment, to be present and live in joy and abundance.
- Stay loyal to those who have supported you through the journey.
- Care for others, have compassion no matter the other persons circumstance's, may they be rich or poor, drug addicts, thieves, murders or not.
- Be strong-minded, remembering what I want so I do not fall into temptations.
- Be aware of my circumstances, take care of my health and my wealth.
- Do not condemn or put others down.

What are your morals and principles?

My moral and principles are:

_____

_____

_____

_____

_____

_____

_____

_____

_____

_____

_____

_____

_____

_____

_____

_____

_____

_____

_____

_____

_____

_____

_____

_____

_____

_____

_____

_____

_____

_____

Revaluate ideas about money!

Stop thinking rich people are greedy and everything was given to them. If you think so, how are you allowed to receive your fortunes? "Rich people steal, cheat and lie!" This isn't necessarily true.

How will you allow yourself to grow in wealth and prosperity while still following your morals and principles?

This is the era of the most self-made millionaires.

Remember, any good foundation is built on integrity and quality or it will not succeed.

Money sayings:

"Money does not grow on trees!"

Money is made from cotton and linen, which comes from the ground and while you are alive you can go out and make it.

"Money is the root of all evil!"

Money will only enhance a person's characteristics, if a person is generous and giving, they will increase in the magnitude in the way they give.

"More money, more problems"

Sure you will have to manage your finances because with less money it is easier to track, but I'd rather cry in a Ferrari than on the train.

"The rich get richer and the poor get poorer"

The correct education can help anyone succeed. The type of education necessary for all may be different. I believe everyone should have financial education, some may need business education to work on their own projects, or school education including sciences, arts and philosophy for certain professions.

All of these sayings and more have been feed in my mind since I was young, now I can change those beliefs and rewrite them.

To rewrite old patterns, let's change the old sayings, making them more positive and let us bring in new money sayings into our lives.

Being rich would not change your morals.

Oprah Winfrey gives so many gifts away. Akon, the rapper, has helped provide many people in African with energy. Many rich people give donations to numerous foundations.

Money does grow from the earth.

While money is being made we can go out and earn what we want.

Poor morals and principles is the root of all evil.

More money, more solutions.

I am not saying money can fix everything, but it can give you time and the capabilities to do things you love; spending time with family and friends, taking that trip, or helping a cause you're passionate about.

Implement sayings like:

"I am a money magnet, money is attracted to me"
"Anywhere I go money follows me"
"I am a magnet for success and good fortune"
"Money flows to me easily, frequently, and abundantly."
"My income is constantly increasing. Money flows easily into life. There is always more than enough"
"I am abundant"
"I am rich"

Many of these affirmations are on my vision board. I had to change my perspective on money, when I did I became more abundant. Now, I attract money instead of chasing it. I do not dwell on the money I spend, I focus on what I have and all my opportunities. I focus on the moment and choose to enjoy the experience. The affirmations help cultivate this mindset.

Let's choose to live a life with high morals and principles. Let us be abundant, knowing there is always enough so we never get greedy. Most of all, let us stop letting misconceptions about money hold us back from the fortunes we believe we deserve and that the world wants to give us.

CHAPTER 5

Power of Belief

What is a belief?

What are limiting beliefs?

How do we destroy limiting beliefs?

Notice the words you use and how they can empower you

WHAT IS A BELIEF?

A belief is the acceptance that something is true or real, a firmly held opinion or conviction.

Our beliefs are our acceptance or perception of a topic that we think is 100% real. Sometimes we take other people's opinion about us or on topics and make it our belief. We have a certain belief of our capabilities, we see society a certain way, and we have our own perceptions on money, politics and religion.

Since we were born, most people are conditioned that the right path is to go to school, do well, get a good job, get married, have kids and live a simple stable life.

We have been fed thoughts on every subject that helped form our beliefs based on others' opinions. We learn our beliefs concerning money, religion, politics and our views on where we stand in society mainly from our parents, friends, school systems, the news, and different television shows and movies.

These perspectives can either weaken us or strengthen us.

Belief is an *acceptance* of something we *think* is true or real.

It is how an individual or group of individuals perceive something. Dr. Wayne Dyer said "If you change the way you look at things, the things you look at change."

We get to decide what we believe.

We get to create and cultivate our own beliefs and cultures.

We can rewrite our own thought patterns for the better. We get to break through our limiting beliefs.

What are Limiting Beliefs?

Our limiting beliefs are developed throughout our lives from our experiences. "I can't be fit because my family and my ancestors are all overweight." "I can't go to college since my parents didn't go to college," or "I have failed so many times; why would this time be any different?" or "If society does not like us then we must be bad people," are examples of limiting beliefs. Educational experiences cultivate our beliefs on our intelligence as well, primarily by making students think that if they do poorly on a test, then they aren't smart or if they fail certain classes then they won't succeed in life. The American education system is designed so there is a low chance of success and a high chance of failure which has a hugely negative impact on students that remains with them long after they leave school. Remember that these things are limiting beliefs: things we *think* are real; they are not *facts*.

We then build excuses around limiting beliefs. "I will not succeed because I did not do well in school." "I could never be rich because of where I come from." Fear helps drive these limiting beliefs, preventing us from changing our circumstances and from achieving our dreams.

Limiting beliefs may not be in the forefront of our mind; they're usually embedded in our deep subconscious.

Examples of some more limiting beliefs we need to let go of:

- I lack motivation.
- I procrastinate too much.
- I don't have time.
- I don't have resources.
- It's too late to change.
- I have too many responsibilities.
- I do not know where to start.

We can become aware of our limiting beliefs and destroy them by choosing to think differently.

DESTROY LIMITING BELIEFS

We have the option to destroy our limiting beliefs and change the way our minds have been conditioned. We get to create unlimited beliefs. We get to change the story we have been telling ourselves and write a brand new one that will empower us and drive our vision.

We can change our story by changing the way we talk.

There are many millionaires, such as Henry Ford, John D. Rockefeller, Steve Jobs, and Richard Branson that did not do well in school. School education does not determine our success. Do not let the education system limit your belief of success. Many people who come from a poor background can make it big. A prime example would be Oprah Winfrey; she had so many struggles and she keep pushing through.

Let's look at some words and phrases that we use in our everyday lives and see how we can change that dialogue in a positive way

It is hard to eat healthy.	Eating healthy *is a challenge I have not yet mastered*
I *can't* fix my diet.	I *can* make better food choices.
I *want* things to work out.	I *choose* to make things work.
I *hate* fast food.	I *prefer* eating healthy.
I *hope* to buy my mom a house.	I *trust* that I will buy my mom a house.
I *try* to eat healthy.	I *do* eat healthy.

LIMITING WORDS EMPOWERING WORDS

The impact of changing these simple words like this will impact your mind, allowing you to be more determined to get what you want.

Let's go over some sayings to build positivity and empower our minds!

"I CAN overcome any obstacle."

"I CAN do anything I put my mind to."

"I CHOOSE to be joyous, wealthy, free, and abundant."

"I CHOOSE to live a lifetime of happiness."

"I TRUST myself to achieve my wildest dreams AND I can do anything I set my mind to."

"I INTEND to go out into the world and have my visions turnout regardless of how I thought I would get there"

When we notice ourselves or anyone around us using words that may be limiting their beliefs, let's show them how they can cultivate their mind with simple adjustments. By supporting other individuals, we will enhance our change of mindset from limiting beliefs to a mindset where anything is possible, if we are willing to have it turn out.

THE POWER OF BELIEF AND HOW WE CAN CULTIVATE THEM

Beliefs can limit us or empower us.

Oprah Winfrey, Jay-Z, Eric Thomas, and many others strongly believe in themselves, so when they were judged and turn down that did not deter them; instead they keep pushing through. Oprah was told she was no good for television, no company wanted to sign Jay-Z, and Eric Thomas was homeless and ate out of garbage cans, but they all believed in themselves. Now Eric Thomas's voice motivates me to go after my dreams.

Henry Ford said, "If you think you can do a thing or you think you can't, you are right."

If you believe you can achieve something, you can and if you don't, then you will not.

I never thought about writing a book so early in my life. I was going to wait until I had more successes under my belt and then tell my story. However, I realized how much I have grown and how my mindset has shifted from anxiety and depression. Now, I can see how I can achieve all my dreams. I wrote this book so as I continue to grow, others can join or enhance their practices on the journey of living in the here and now as well. Together, we can reduce greed and create what we want to see in the world.

I've moved myself away from a mentality of self-doubt and fear, which is a process that I continue daily. When you take time to connect with yourself outside of work, school and other responsibilities of life, you are able to be in the now, which can be a big challenge with all the distractions around you. Then you have the opportunity to experience the blissful part of life and be grateful for what you have. I have grown through self-development books, audios, and workshops all of which encouraged me to start counting my wins and talk to myself as the champion that I am. We are all kings and queens; we just have to accept the blessings and opportunities that we get in life. I have cultivated my practices of exercise, chanting, meditation and my practice of gratitude, allowing myself to appreciate life, all that I have, and all the things I can do to help.

In *The Secret*, they say "ask, believe, receive." The Secret explains the power of asking for what you want, believing you deserve it, and allowing yourself to receive what you ask for.

For me, the hardest part is belief.

After setting goals, watching my productivity, and doing my meditative exercises, I realized the reason that I don't receive is either that I don't believe I deserve it or I am not fully open to receiving what I want.

Am I accepting what I ask for? Is it what I truly want? Do I believe that I deserve it? Am I allowing the world the chance to give me these things?

What I learned was I need to relax and quiet my mind in order to change my mindset.

We have to give the mind the chance to shift and with all the noise from outside, the mind struggles to break past the current beliefs and drown out the noise. When the mind is relaxed and quieted through exercise and meditative practices, we then allow our beliefs to manifest.

How can you cultivate your beliefs? Feed your mind. Override what is limiting you. Practice positive affirmations and stick with your growth and meditative practices.

EXAMPLES OF POSITIVE AFFIRMATIONS:

"I am receiving health, wealth, intelligence, strength, possibilities and opportunities in abundance in my life right now."

"I am capable of love."
"I am full of love and joy and I exuberate it all around me."
"I am strong."

"I am beautiful."
"I am powerful."
"I deserve all that I ask for."
"I am highly blessed and everything is working in my favor."
"Everything will work out for the best."
"I am all I need."

Repeat these to yourself whenever you may need a reminder that you are strong and capable and that you have the potential and abilities to do whatever you want.

Choose your positive affirmations and repeat them daily:

_____

_____

_____

_____

_____

_____

_____

_____

_____

_____

Meditation allows your mind to expand and kill the needless tangents. Exercise increases your self-esteem and self-confidence. Chanting helps overwrite repeated worries that flow in our head from all that we're exposed to on a daily basis. Above all else, be grateful for where you are, where you came from, all that you have, and all your abilities to go out and get what you want.

The transition happens when we learn to be in the present moment because no moment will ever be as great as the one you're in right now.

Whatever challenges you, destroy that anxiety and conquer that fear. Make your phone calls, finally talk to that person you've wanted to talk to, run that marathon.

If something scares you, go for it, and do not look back. Have the experiences you dream of.

Keep your rituals and good practices high and remind yourself to be grateful and appreciate where you are. Your increased awareness will allow you to see your true strengths and gifts, allowing you to go out into the world and make what you want happen.

CHAPTER 6

Routines and Rituals

Why is it important to get into positive habits
and make sure you repeat them?

Positive routines and rituals help keep you on track to achieve
your goals, maintain your health, and reduce stress, allowing
you to go wholeheartedly after the life you dream of.

As my practice continues and becomes stronger, I become
stronger. I see all the things I focus on come to fruition. I
started getting more into action towards my goals and purpose
with less fear and more confidence. I realized I am not just
lucky, I am blessed. I remind my self that no matter what
happens, "I will be successful because I am determined to keep
going and get what I want."

Most highly successful people have daily routines to keep them
on track. Statistics from *Forbes* show what these routines entail:
exercise 59%, family time 41%, e-mails 36%, meditation 10%,
pet time 9%, reading 6% and music 5%.

Some people have nightly rituals as well, so consider whatever
works best for you.

I believe it is best to have daily rituals. If daily rituals don't fit
well with your schedule then aim to keep your positives higher
than your negatives; meaning that your goal should be to practice
your routines for 4 out of the 7 days, so you reached the target 4

times for the 3 days you didn't. Personally, I strive for all 7 days, but remember to not take life too seriously. Don't stress yourself out with something that is supposed to help you maintain peace.

When doing these processes, remember to enjoy the moment and realize you are doing this for yourself and your own well-being. Tell your mind this feels great and I am fortunate to have this opportunity.

According to Forbes, many successful people get up meditate, have positive affirmations, listen to motivational videos, spend time with their ones, handle major tasks and exercise. This is what I call PAYING YOURSELF FIRST.

Some other tips:

- Put your phone on do not disturb or silent, as long as you can hear your alarm in the morning.
- Include greens in your daily diet.
- Move your body.
- Meditate to increase your awareness.
- Plan your day beforehand, either the night before or the morning of.
- Journal when you feel it is appropriate, some say at night and others say after meditation. Journal consistently. Log your goals and see what you have been up to; it's a great way to motivate yourself and stay on track.
- Get your day started early; less people are up, and you'll get more peace and quiet.
- Listen to more positive words in the morning because when you first wake up, your mind is more receptive to what it hears.

This is my daily routine:

- Wake up
- Say three things I am grateful for. "Thank you for life and all my opportunities. Thank you for my family and friends. Thank you for protecting me through the night and keeping me healthy and strong."
- Say three positive affirmations. "I love all and all love me. I am a strong, beautiful, confident, caring and powerful man. I am abundant and blessed and everything I do is working in my favor."
- Drink 2 glasses of water and do a quick 2 to 3 minute stretch.
- Meditate for 20 minutes while chanting (or chant throughout the day).
- Exercise 15 to 20 minutes (unless I have a gym session planned).
- Listen to uplifting audios while I shower.
- Get dressed.
- Make a shake or have cereal/oatmeal.
- Various day-to-day activities.
- Nighttime 5-minute journal. Write down major tasks to work on the next day.
- 15-20 minutes of meditation.
- Say something I am grateful for on each bead of my 108 mala bead necklace.

What positive habits would you like to apply and when?

Habits/Activities	Time (Morning/midday/night)

Routines create positive habits, that help you care for your own well-being. We can only give what we have, so we have to cultivate our own joy and mindset of abundance. Practices specific to you will allow the joy, compassion, and abundance to flow into your life and spread to all those around you.

My routines allow me to always be in a state of appreciation, finding the good in everything. Even when that guys cuts me off in traffic, I breath and remind myself life is great. I am enthusiastic and say hi to as many people as I can and spread love and compliments. I feel the radiation of love continually growing inside of me. It helps me to have better relationships with my family, friends and all the people I encounter. The love is also generated by my practice of constantly sending out good vibes and energy to all the people I know personally and the world.

Find a routine that works for you and let it enhance your journey!

CHAPTER 7

Mindset Shift to Abundance

What does it mean to live in abundance?

Where does it originate from?

How do we cultivate our mindset to abundance?

Abundance is having a copious amount of something, and prosperity in all aspects of life. Abundance originates from a place of love once we realize when we have enough and that we can do more than we imagine, we are able to live in a life of contribution. Abundance leads to gratitude, trust, love, self-worth, and generosity. On the other hand, we have scarcity, which originates from fear. Scarcity is when there is not enough and the fear that you cannot have what you want.

Let us raise our awareness with mindsets associated with both scarcity and abundance. Allow yourself to let go of fear and scarcity, welcoming and embracing love and abundance.

The awareness has allowed me to shift my mindset to abundance, helping me to keep a positive attitude. This allows me to see the different ways I can have my goals turn out, enabling me to continuously be in the present moment and spread joy, love, and compassion.

Mindsets of scarcity: people who criticize, hold grudges, have a sense of entitlement, take all the credit for collective victories, blame others for their failures, think they know it all, watch television every day, fear change, talk about people, horde information and data, secretly hope others fail, and never set goals.

A scarcity mindset only thinks about short term goals, which limits their mindset and can hurt their finances. In scarcity, you don't trust people or systems because you think there's not enough of anything. This is a big reason why people binge eat and/or steal, due to fear of shortage. Scarcity builds insecurities and self-doubt, which may cause sadness, jealousy, and cheating.

I lived in a scarcity mindset for a long time. A place where I could not even trust my own parents, feeling they wanted all my money and time. I did not trust women due to seeing them cheat on their own husbands. I got overweight because deep down in my subconscious mind, I ate as much as I could because I feared shortage. It was a horrible feeling to always think I did not have enough, exhausting myself and my mind by overworking to get more. I was always cautious, not allowing me to be myself and express joy.

A scarcity mindset is always ready to come up. We have to choose to see abundance, focusing on all that we have and all that we can choose to be. When we focus on the positives, we allow more positive things to enter our life.

An abundant mindset is where the joy starts flowing in. Abundant mindsets are associated with giving compliments to others as well as ourselves and having a sense of gratitude for all your opportunities. This mindset allows you to forgive others, give other people credit for shared victories, keep a journal, want others to succeed, talk about ideas, share information and data, set goals, and develop plans.

Abundance comes from realizing that there is enough for you to help yourself and to help others, allowing you to share and give without the need to get something in return. Abundance allows you to trust others as well as yourself and to become grateful for all your experiences and see everything from a positive perspective. Best of all, from an abundance mindset you want the best for others *and* yourself.

The first part of shifting is realizing that our mindsets originate from within and they are cultivated from our habits and our thoughts. We have to relax our mind, reduce stress, and experience every moment, so we can see how good life is. We can stop thinking about past regrets and losses. Instead, we can look at the lessons we learned and all the good times we had. For the future, we can stop thinking about what we might achieve and what may not happen and start focusing on all the ways things can turn out even better than we imagined. This is what I call broadening your vision. Abundance allows you to focus on the long term, giving yourself a chance to create plans, allowing you to set goals to go out after what you want and to create the vision you want. When you think on a long-term basis that allows you to weigh different options and their benefits or consequences. In the mindset of abundance, you create positive feelings towards everyone, allowing you to build trust and see the good in others, along with the good in yourself.

To feel abundance is such a relief. I am able to trust people, even people I do not know. Do not get me wrong, I am not naïve, I have wisdom on my side to not be taken advantage of. The break through is I am able to be vulnerable and love people whole heartedly. I love on my family and friends. I even let an amazing woman in my life. When my mindset shifted, I see how everyone around me is trying to support me. I am more enthusiastic about life. I now help people more freely, without expecting anything in return. When I started setting goals, my achievements increased and so did my happiness.

I am building more compassion and spreading joy through my meditative practices. I am volunteering in meditation workshops and spreading knowledge and support in health, wellness and finance. This feeling is wonderful and no words can give is justice, it is total freedom. I lost 25 pounds in a healthy manner and I stopped eating my midnight meals. I am now in a state of gratitude for all my experiences in life, all the people in my life and all the opportunities. I am achieving more than I ever dreamed of and my optimism is high. Everything in life is going smooth, remembering what we focus on expands. My routines and rituals allowed me to make this shift of mindset.

How to Cultivate the Mindset

When having conversations with friends and family, talk about things you both appreciate in life and why. In this process, you build gratitude and explore your personal experience and successes as well as the other person's.

Become more organized at home and in your daily life. When you start cleaning up and reducing your clutter, the noise in your mind decreases and you create space. The things you want have more room and you can accept new opportunities. When you start observing and creating a schedule, you start seeing the amount of time you have. You become more efficient and you can incorporate new activities you may not have had time for before.

Reduce the outside noise to remind yourself of what you truly want, your intuition. Listen to what's going on in your mind. Do not get lost in activities that don't help you grow or forge connections with others. When you use your time more efficiently that allows you to start on projects you have been putting off.

Giving is receiving, so share what you have with others. When you start to contribute outwardly, you become the change you want to see in the world. Make sure that all you do is a win-win situation for all parties involved and/or affected. When I say win-win, I am not reffering to keeping count. The term means to make sure whatever you may be doing benefits the other. Do not create a tally and feel others owe you. Give from an unconditional place of contribution. Remember to give means you have to be willing to receive as well. If you do not receive and accept things people are giving you, you end up breaking the cycle of giving and receiving.

When a situation arises look for positives. "What can I learn from this situation?" This helps you in a growth mindset.

Change how you verbally approach a situation. Instead of saying "I have to do this," say, "I choose to do this." It helps liberate your mind and bring joy to the table.

More than anything *do not* compare yourself to others. Love yourself and all that you are. Know who you are and the heart that you have.

You *get* to be the change you want to see in the world.

Create your rituals and practices.

Help yourself by feeding your mind with encouragement and positivity. Use vision boards, covering all your topics of interest, finances, well-being, family and friends, health, and trips just to name a few. Even have more than one vision board if you want.

Listen to motivational audios and read self-help books. Remember that there is *nothing* wrong with asking for or admitting that you need support.

Read books that will empower you. Develop your meditative practices and see where you could build rituals and routines into your life so it brings you joy.

Living in the now allows your dreams to manifest. Now is the only moment you have. you cannot change the past or control the future. The only time is NOW. Being present is what allows us to be in a mindset of abundance, knowing that we have enough. Further filling us with joy, love and compassion, enabling us to spread it to all those around us.

Keep going on your path and let abundance wash over you.

CPSIA information can be obtained
at www.ICGtesting.com
Printed in the USA
FSOW01n2356271017
40418FS